HOW TO CREATE A REAL SPELL BOOK

Your Guide to Writing Wiccan Spells and Witchcraft Rituals

By Didi Clarke

Disclaimer:
While I have performed all these spells myself, your results may vary.

CONTENTS

By Didi Clarke

*If you'd like to be notified when I publish a new book or have something exciting in the works, be sure to sign up for my mailing list. You'll receive a **FREE** color magick correspondence chart when you do! Follow this link to subscribe:*

https://mailchi.mp/01863952b9ff/didi-clarke-mailing-list

CHAPTER 1: WELCOME TO THE WORLD OF SPELL WRITING

As a witch, performing a spell is one of the most exciting and invigorating events you can experience. But did you know there's something even more exhilarating waiting for you in the world of witchcraft?

Performing spells—*that you wrote yourself!*

While we witches respect the traditions and magick that have been handed down to us, we're also quite a DIY bunch. This means you'll find plenty of witches, Wiccans, pagans, and other practitioners creating their own spells and working their own magick.

And something tells me you might be a tiny bit interested in spell writing too!

Introducing How to Create a Real Spell Book!

Discovering the limits of the spiritual world. Increasing your capacity for creativity. Sharing your passion for Wicca with the world.

These are just a few of the many reasons why witches begin writing their own spells. But the process isn't as simple as deciding to do it—there's a definite art to spell writing, and like any skill, you've got to learn the basics and master the fundamentals.

How to Create a Real Spell Book is here to teach you that art!

I've been crafting my own spells for years now, and I'm excited to get to share my process with you. Every witch must develop their own unique spell writing style, but it's my hope that by showing you my own personal tips, tricks, techniques, and struggles, you'll develop a solid foundation from which to build your own craft!

What You'll Find in This Book

How to Create a Real Spell Book is broken down into two primary parts.

Part One

In part one, we're taking a look at the art of spell writing itself. These are the steps I use myself when crafting a new ritual or spell. In this section, you'll learn things like:

- Brainstorming ideas
- Arranging the elements of your spell
- Different spell types
- How to measure your results
- Common pitfalls to avoid

This is a lot of information to take it, so I recommend taking your time and taking notes. And don't be afraid to go back and re-read sections you don't quite understand!

Like I said, this is my process, and while it ultimately may be different from the one you develop, it's important to understand the spell writing basics that are being laid out here.

Part Two

The second part of this book is meant to act as a reference guide as you begin to write your own spells. These late chapters are filled with correspondences—which are the building blocks of any good spell.

A correspondence is any item or concept that has a spiritual association. We use them to create a link between the mysterious, ethereal spirit world and our own tangible physical world. Choosing objects with the correct spiritual associations is key to creating spells that have a noticeable effect on the world around us.

For example, take the color red. Witches and non-witches alike frequently associate this color with love. So, we can say that red corresponds (or shares a correspondence) with love. For this reason, we might include red objects in love spells or other magick associated with romance.

This is just one example, but all correspondences function this way. That's why it's important to have a big list of them to pull ideas from.

In the correspondence chapters, you'll find my personal correspondence tables that I use in my own spell writing. Pretty much any object or idea under the sun can have a correspondence, but I've included some of the most popular and important ones in witchcraft.

These include correspondences for:
- Colors
- Numbers
- Moon Phases
- Plants
- Days of the Week
- Wiccan Holidays

Choosing the right combination of these will help focus your intentions and magnify your results.

Let's Begin Our Spell Writing Journey

Enough with the introductions—it's time to get to the good stuff!

Are you ready to explore the world of spell writing for yourself?

Let's get started!

CHAPTER 2: DEVELOPING YOUR SPELL INTENTION AND BRAINSTORMING CORRESPONDENCES

As you become more experienced at writing your own spells, there are two problems you'll frequently run into—you've got more ideas that you know what to do with or you haven't got a single one at all!

Both of these can be frustrating in their own way. Trying to wrangle your racing thoughts is just as much of a challenge as trying to come up with one when it feels like your imagination is a barren desert.

In this chapter, we're going to take a look at my process for creating a starting point, or intention, for a spell and using that as a way to brainstorm correspondences that relate to that intention. Whether you've got too many ideas to handle or have a serious case of writer's block, this is the place to begin.

Step 1: Determine your intention.

Whether it's spell writing or anything else you want to do in life, you've got to start somewhere.

Maybe there's a type of spell you've always wanted to try writing. Something like plant magick or crystal magick. Starting from a particular branch of magick is one way to begin the spell writing process.

But it's not the only way!

Maybe instead there's a particular topic you're interested in creating a spell for. Something like a love spell or a money spell or a good luck spell. This is another perfectly fine place to start the process!

Narrowing the Magickal Field

The point of this process is to start general and get specific. So, as you find a general point of interest—like love spells or plant magick—you should begin to narrow your focus until a spell intention comes into view.

To show you what I mean about getting specific, let's take the two previous examples, love spells and plant magick.

Already, we're getting pretty specific for these two things—you've got a plant-based love spell so far! However, it still lacks an intention—that specific purpose that gives a spell life. So more specific we shall go!

Now let's say you find yourself getting a little tongue-tied and nervous on first dates, so you want this spell to focus on improving those. That means this spell should focus on things like creating charisma, charm, and conversational skills within yourself.

And there's your intention that completes the first step of the process! You've not got a plant-based love spell to help you be more charming on a first date. And that's something we can work with.

A Final Note on This Step

This first step shouldn't be a stressful, intense affair. It's simply about helping you clearly lay out some of the options available to you. Nothing has to be set in stone and nothing has to be done immediately—these are your absolute first steps into the world of spell writing!

If you're struggling for ideas, go as basic and broad as you need to get the job done. If you're full of potential starting points—jot down as many as you like. Keep in mind that you probably won't be able to use them all for a single spell, but it's always nice to have them in one place for future reference.

Step 2: Create a correspondence brain dump.

In step two, we're turning our starting point into a jumping off point. It's now time for a brain dump!

As much as I hate how that word sounds, it's an excellent process for refining and developing your spell ideas. In a nutshell, you're going to be jotting down every possible correspondence associated with your spell intention.

Don't hold anything back during this process—it's 100% about quantity over quality! You'll go back through and narrow down what you've got later, but the whole point of a brain dump is about giving yourself plenty of material to sift through and work with.

This is the step of the spell writing process where those correspondence tables later in the book will really come in handy. I recommend keeping them close by as you move through this process.

Here's an example to show you what I mean:

Let's go back to our plant-based love spell for charm on a first date. That means you want everything in your brain dump to be related to that topic.

So, let's start listing off some ideas.

In terms of colors, you've got red and pink—those are commonly associated with love. Roses are a good flower choice for love, but there are also forget-me-nots (for memorable experiences), ginger (for charm), cayenne (for speaking skills), and a whole host of other possible plants.

The number two is a number of love, so it should go in the brain dump too—as well as Tuesdays, Fridays, and the full moon phase.

That was just a short example—this process can go on for a while. And it should!

Like I mentioned before, the whole point of a brain dump is to give yourself plenty of raw material to work with. Most of this will end up on the cutting room floor, but it's much easier to eliminate ideas you don't need than create ideas where there are none.

When doing your own brain dump, don't forget to think about all possible correspondences. This step is really about stretching the limits of your imagination. These correspondences can include:
- Colors
- Numbers
- Days of the Week
- Holidays
- Moon Phases
- Plants
- Crystals
- Gods & Goddesses
- Astrological signs
- Chakras
- Planets
- Whatever else you can come up with!

During a brain dump, there's no such thing as a bad idea—so jot down everything that comes to mind! I suggest creating a simple list for this process. You can try to categorize the list items if you like, but really, that process comes in later steps. Right now, just worry about getting everything down.

A short, simple explanation for your items (e.g. "ginger—charm" or "lilies—faithfulness") can also be beneficial when reviewing your brain dump later.

Step 3: Narrow down your options.

By this point in the process, you should have a massively long list of possible correspondences and associations. But there's no way that all of it will fit into a single spell!

Now comes the hard part—narrowing things down to only the most essential elements.

When your mind is full of great ideas, it can be hard to get rid of any of them, but always remember that we don't narrow our spells down to restrict ourselves. Instead, we do it to make our spells as potent as possible. The more singular your focus is, the more of a spiritual punch your magick will pack.

Plus, you can always return to those great ideas at a later time for even more spells!

When it comes to winnowing away everything but the essentials, there are no ironclad laws about what you should be left with. However, when I'm making my own spells, this is the general area I aim for:

- 2 to 4 objects that best encapsulate my goal (these should form a somewhat logical group)
- A single color or color scheme that represents my goal (I want something spiritually powerful but also visually pleasing)
- A specific day or moon phase that will enhance my magick (planning spells becomes more complicated as you add conditional elements like these)
- A deity or other spiritual entity to invoke (this is optional, and you should always use caution when invoking)

Spells come in all shapes and sizes, but when you're just starting out writing your own, this is a good ideal to aim for. As you gain more experience and learn more about your abilities, you will probably begin to branch out, but a list like this will provide you with a manageable and closely related set of correspondences to work with.

If you're having trouble finding the correspondences you want to use, keep these two tips in mind: look for themes and think about logistics.

Look for themes.

If you've already got a few correspondences picked out, looking for a common theme can be a great way to incorporate some more supplemental elements into your spell.

Let's back up and try a more general love spell example this time:

Say you're certain you want to incorporate roses but aren't sure what else. A couple theme options come to mind with just that one item!

For one, you could try a natural theme and incorporate other objects that are plant-based like roses. This might be a great opportunity for a tincture—which is a solution that distills the spiritual energies of plants into liquid form.

However, you could also go with an elemental theme. A rose represents the earth, so all you would need are items that have an association with love and represent air, water, and fire—the other three elements within Wicca.

When doing this work, the point isn't to find the "correct" theme, but rather, it's about developing an eye for catching on to themes in general. Anything you can do to promote the unity and focus of your magick will intensify its effects.

Think about logistics.

It's important not to stifle your creativity during this process, but at the same time, you do need to look at your list with a practical, logistical eye as well. Because what's the point of writing a spell if you can't even perform it?

That giant ring of candles might sound cool on paper, but arranging and lighting all 1000 of them would take hours! You might like three different types of incense billowing out under your bedroom door, but your roommate with allergies might disagree!

There are lots of practical, everyday constraints like time, resources, and the feelings of others that limit our magick in certain ways. In most cases, it pays to work with these constraints, not against them—like I said, what's the point of writing a spell that you won't have an opportunity to perform?

But it's important to remember that these things aren't holding you back—they're actually improving your skills. All of these logistical problems require workarounds, which means that your creativity and cunning are going to get a serious workout. And these are two skills that every spell writer needs plenty of!

Step 4: Allow the spell to come into focus in its own time.

Because of the excitement in the spell writing process, it can be hard to be patient and allow the elements of your spells to show themselves when they're ready. But a patient mindset is exactly what's needed!

If you're struggling to come up with the perfect combination of correspondences for your spell, don't try to rush the process by throwing in stuff just for the sake of having something. Don't settle for good enough—allow the great stuff to make itself known.

Sometimes this patience takes the form of being meticulous and carefully evaluating all of your options. Other times—especially if you're struggling with complete writer's block—it's best to shelve the spell for a day, a week, a month, a year, or even longer. Please believe me when I say that having no spell is better than a having hasty, forced one!

We all know that magick doesn't work on our schedule. It moves according to its own timeline. But the same is true for the spell writing process. Sometimes you've got to wait for the right opportunity to present itself to you, but you're likely to miss it if you don't have patience and trust in the process.

CHAPTER 3: STRUCTURING YOUR SPELL

B y now, you've got all the elements of a great spell, but what to do with them? Throwing whatever you've got at the universe and seeing what sticks is a terrible way to practice magick! You've got to combine your correspondences with some kind of action and order to create and cast a proper spell.

The next goal in our spell writing process is to give your spell some structure in terms of the actions you're performing. As you read spells from a wide variety of authors (which is something I highly recommend you do), you'll begin to naturally discover the many different ways a spell can unfold.

But if you're new to the world of spell writing or witchcraft in general, you might not have that personal experience to fall back on. And that's where templates come in handy!

What is a Template?

A template is simply pre-determined way to structure your spell that's tried and true and shown to be effective. For those of you who would rather wander off the beaten path, there's absolutely nothing wrong with creating a structure from scratch. But I know personally that in the early days of your spell writing, there are lots of things to keep track of. Spell templates are a way to simplify what can be a very confusing process.

In this chapter, I'm going to show you three different spell templates. Undoubtedly, there are many different types of spells that I missed, but I find myself returning to these three the most.

First, we'll look a good general set up for shorter spells that don't require many (if any) supplies. Next, we'll look at a longer ritual format that can accommodate more of your "bells and whistles." Finally, we'll take a look at invocation rituals, which require some special spell elements and should be approached with the utmost care.

Short Spell Template

When I say "short spells", I'm thinking of something close to the stereotypical "spells" that you see witches casting in popular media. They're snappy, they usually rhyme, and involve only the barest of essentials when it comes to items. I can say that I condone of all the "magick" portrayed in TV and movies, but there's a kernel of truth there when it comes to these types of spells—magick doesn't always have to be flashy or incredibly complex.

Short spells like these are a great starting point for three types of witches:
- Beginners (because of their simplicity)
- Folks who don't want to use a ton of items (because of their convenience)
- And folks who love to write (because they're very word- and rhyme-heavy)

When it comes to the basic layout of a short spell, there's not much to take in. You've got the following:
- 3 to 4 lines that you're going to recite
- A single action that you perform while reciting the lines or immediately afterward

Don't let this simple template fool you, though! Because of its brevity and simplicity, choosing the correct words, actions, and items is of the utmost importance. You've only got one chance to get things right.

My best advice would be to start simple and build from there. Start with a spell where you say a couple lines and light a candle. Or try one where you whistle a short melody! Strangely enough, whistling is great for spells where you're trying to attract positive spiritual energy.

Trust your creative intuition, but don't be afraid to pare things down to the basics when it comes to these short spells. They're perfect for small, everyday magickal tasks that don't warrant an entire ritual.

Ritual Spell Template

For those times when you want to create a spell that involves more moving parts and packs more of a punch, use this ritual spell template. It will help take you from start to finish with your own magickal creations! This is the format you will most commonly see in my spells and books.

Protection

To begin with, every ritual should always open with some sort of protective measure. For many witches, this means casting a sacred circle—and if you want to use your own casting technique for this section, that works completely. However, a sacred circle is not your only option.

Instead, I will sometimes opt to call upon the spirits of the four cardinal directions (north, south, east, and west) for protection. Or if you have other entities or energies you work with, it's fine to ask protection from them as well. As long as your words, actions, and correspondences all point towards protection, it will shine through in your spell.

Blessing

Next up comes the blessing of the items.

Now, there are some general tools, like wands or bells, that many witches will use across multiple spells. Typically, these items should be blessed beforehand.

However, if you've got any ritual-specific items you're using, this is the time to bless them.

My go-to technique for blessing is to allow a bowl of water to sit under the moonlight for three hours. When it's time for the ritual, I will use the water to anoint the items to be blessed. Additionally, I may ask the spirits of the water to cleanse the item or I may ask for a blessing from the Triple Goddess, since she is associated with the moon.

However, as with the protective measures, your only goal in this section is to promote blessing energies through words, actions, and items. I highly encourage you to branch out and see what blessing techniques you can come up with on your own!

Body

Now we come to the actual body of the spell. This is where the magick happens!

Once again, this is an opportunity for you to be creative. As you're sitting down to write this part, make sure that the intention of your spell is clear in your mind. And if you find yourself getting overwhelmed with options, remember to toss anything that doesn't strongly contribute towards that intention.

I couldn't possibly predict all of the interesting spell topics you're coming up with, but I would like to provide just a few basic techniques that I return to frequently in my own spell writing:

- Burn incense to banish energy
- Burn candles to draw in energy
- Ring a bell to summon a spirit guide or familiar
- Move clockwise to generate energy
- Move counterclockwise to release energy you've generated
- Use knots to combine the energies of different objects

Now, none of these are hard and fast rules—I use candles to banish energy sometimes, and, in my opinion, there's never a bad time to ring a bell. What's important is that you experiment and find what works for your, so that you can begin to develop an internal consistency to your spell writing.

And as always, no matter what your objects and actions are supposed to represent, be sure that the words you're using help reinforce these representations that you've chosen.

Conclusion

No matter how and intense or exciting the body of your spell may have been, it's always important to tie things up with a concluding section.

The main focus of this section is to close your sacred circle (if you opened one) and to thank and release any spirits or energies you may have called on—for protection or for any other reason.

At the very end of your spell, it's also a nice idea to reiterate your desire one final time before you officially conclude the ritual.

Invocations

For the uninitiated, an invocation is a spell meant to summon, communicate with, or petition a deity. Because gods and goddesses are highly powerful, highly intelligent spiritual beings, you should always approach writing invocations with caution, care, and respect.

Ritual Layout

In terms of the actual layout of an invocation, they can be similar to that of a normal ritual. This is especially true if your goal is to ask a deity for assistance or communicate with them more generally.

For the most part, I will suggest leaving the ritual template largely intact for invocations. However, there is one important addition you need to make—the actual invocation of the deity.

Commonly, this will take place after the blessing of objects but before the body of the ritual. This invocation can also completely replace the body of the spell, if that fits better with your intention.

This section should begin with some sort of prayer or praise to the deity. Specific gods and traditions often have specific rules and techniques for invoking, so be sure to research your chosen god or goddess thoroughly before you start writing.

For gods that are known to be kind and just, this prayer doesn't need to be excessive. Honestly stating your respect and desire for communion should be enough to satisfy them. For more...fickle deities, a little extra charm and praise might be necessary. (Once again, this is why it's so important to do your research!)

In addition to your prayer, you will need to come up with some sort of offering to the god or goddess. Some have specific gifts they require, while others will accept any object related to them and their correspondences.

Once the prayer is complete, you should add a short section that states your intentions for invoking the deity. Be clear and concise in this section to ensure your results are as expected.

At this point, the ritual can continue as normal with any other actions and objects you may have planned.

Additionally, when you reach the conclusion of your invocation ritual, the deity should always be bid farewell first before any other beings or energies. And always reiterate your thanks for their assistance in your spell!

CHAPTER 4: COMMON PITFALLS IN SPELL WRITING

L ike anything, learning to write a good spell takes patience and practice. You can read as many books on the subject as you'd like, but nothing beats experience as a teacher. However, there are some problems that commonly crop up with first-time spell writers.

In this chapter, we're going to be taking a look at some of the frequent pitfalls and other issues that can hinder your progress with creating your own spells. For one reason or another, it's these issues that seem to cause the most friction in the process.

Pitfall #1: Being a Perfectionist Right Out of the Gate

We all obviously want our spells to be as polished as possible, but when you're just starting out with this art, there are a TON of elements you're trying to juggle in your mind. Correspondences, actions, lines—these all are demanding your attention, and for a newbie, it can be hard to keep them all in order!

So, when it comes to those first few spells you write, try not to think of them as perfect specimens ready to share with the world. Instead, think of them as learning experiences meant hone your skills and refine your process. None of us—not even me—end up with an excellent spell on our first try.

For those of us with perfectionist tendencies, this can be hard to hear. We're used to getting it right and getting it right out of the gate! But this is one instance where you need to trust the process and improve along the way.

I promise, one day those super-polished, phenomenal spells will flow from your fingertips with ease. But before that, you've got to get a grasp on how all these moving parts come together to make magick.

Pitfall #2: Not Learning From Others

All the best poets read a wide variety of poetry. All the best filmmakers watch different kinds of films. So why wouldn't a good spell writer need to read spells too?

Reading to gain new experience may seem obvious, but you'd be surprised at how many witches skip this step and dive straight into spell writing without seeing what's out there. But it's MUCH harder to write spells without some sort of reference point to guide you.

(Obviously this doesn't apply to you, dear reader, or you wouldn't have picked up a book about spell writing in the first place!)

Reading spells from a wide variety of witches and traditions is essential for uncovering all the opportunities available to you. Some authors will benefit you by introducing you to new techniques you'll want to try. Some authors will benefit you by introducing you to new techniques that you want no part of.

You don't have to enjoy every spell you read—that's not the point. The point is to expand your magickal imagination and show you what other active spell writers are up to.

Pitfall #3: Not Measuring Your Results

In the next chapter, we're going to look at some specific way to measure results, but for now all you need to know is this: measure your results!

Obviously magick isn't science, so there's no need to go overboard. But if the point of magick is to manipulate physical and spiritual energy, why in the world would you not want to know if your spells are missing the mark or not?

Keeping track of the ways your spells influence the world around you is essential to improving. Seeing what works and what doesn't allows you to make tweaks and adjustments until your magick is providing more hits than misses.

It's impossible to optimize your spell-writing abilities to the point that everything you write works perfectly 100% of the time, but it is absolutely possible to make real, tangible improvements to your craft.

But you'll never know if you're improving or not if you don't keep track!

Pitfall #4: Spreading Yourself Too Thin

Plant magick, invocations, candle magick, charms, amulets, ritual magick—there are an exciting number of different traditions within the world of witchcraft! And if you're like me, you're tempted to sample a little of them all.

While it's perfectly fine to dabble and experiment—especially if you're a new witch or spell writer—there's an argument to made for specializing in a particular tradition as well.

If you're constantly hopping from tradition to tradition, you're learning a little bit about a lot of things. But to really improve you need nuance and you need a deep understanding—and that's something you'll only find by digging deep into a specific tradition.

I'm not trying to imply that if you choose candle magick (or whatever else) you're locked in for life. But I am most definitely suggesting that you'll learn more by spending some real time learning a specific tradition. Even if you only learn that it's not for you, that's still a valuable lesson to have.

Pitfall #5: Losing the Magic of Magick

Because of the nature of spell writing, you've got to take a very systematic approach to magick. To some degree, you're required to break it down into smaller elements so that you can understand and control it better.

Unfortunately, this approach can lead us to think of witchcraft as some sort of math equation. As long as you plug in all the right stuff, you'll get your desired output, right?

Wrong!

This approach completely disregards, well, the *magic* of magick.

If you're like me, one of the major appeals of witchcraft was its sense of wonder and mystery. It was the idea that there was this ethereal, spiritual realm waiting for us to explore and utilize. When we lose that sense of wonder, we really lose the heart and soul of witchcraft.

Obviously spell writers have to be somewhat practical minded because our art does indeed have a technical aspect to it. However, as your technical abilities increase, never forget the wonder that makes all this hard, technical work worth it.

CHAPTER 5: MEASURING YOUR RESULTS

B y this point, you've heard me mention measuring results several times. This is one of the most important things a spell writer can do, but unfortunately, it's also one of the most common things people skip in the process.

I think a big reason why this is the case it that, for many people, the term "measuring results" conjures of up images of pouring over giant spreadsheets of data or setting up high-tech experiments. Basically, this part of the process feels like a chore.

It would be ridiculous to pretend that measuring results doesn't involve ANY work, but trust me—I promise it's perfectly manageable. It's also essential for improving your spell writing abilities.

Once you see the benefit it provides, you'll be much more motivated to keep up with it!

In this chapter, we're going to be taking a look at some tips, tricks, ideas, and processes you can use to track the results of your own spells. It's not necessary that you adopt all of them, but I highly suggest giving them all a try to see what works best for you and your own style.

Tip #1: Take good notes through the entire spell-writing process.

Keeping your thoughts and ideas recorded and organized will make every step of spell writing that much easier. But it can be particularly important when it comes to measuring results.

Specifically, it's great for when a spell doesn't turn out like you were expecting.

When that happens, one of my first actions is to start at the top of my notes and work my way down. Because I'm able to see each step of the process, it's easier to spot potential places where things might have gone wrong.

I encourage you to experiment with what and how you should be recording, but here are a few essentials I always like to keep in mind:
- Correspondence meanings (and where I found them) for items/objects I'm not super familiar with or for correspondences I borrowed from a book or other source
- Outline of the ritual I'm writing
- A short explanation about why each section of the outline is included (this is particularly important when you return to your spell later and can't remember why you put in a particular step!)
- A description of the spell's intention (so you can compare your results later)

Tip #2: Only test one or two variables at a time.

There will be instances in spell writing where you have multiple options that all seem appealing. A lot of times this crops up when you're trying to choose things like colors or herbs—multiple ones can have similar correspondences.

When this happens, it's the perfect time to test different variations of your spell. For example, you might want to see how it performs if you use a pink candle vs. a dark red candle. However, it's important that you not test too many variables all at once. And there a couple of reasons why this is a good rule to put in place.

For one, it's just going to make measuring your results that much more difficult.

If you're tracking 100 different variables in a spell, you're going to be doing a lot more tracking than you are magick! And that's not at all the point of measuring your success—it's supposed to help you, not burden you.

But testing a lot of variable all at once is also a bad idea because it can be difficult to pinpoint the things that are having a noticeable impact on your spell.

To go back to our 100-variable example—who's to say that tweaking variable 7 is improving your spell when it could be the tweaks to variables 16, 45, or 89? When you only have one or two things changing across different variations of a spell, you can be more confident that these are what are causing the changes.

Tip #3: Have patience with your results.

If you've been practicing magick for any length of time, you know that spells unfold according to their own schedule, not ours. While there are things you can do to influence things like the potency and effectiveness of spells, the precise timing of them is out of our control.

That's why it's always incredibly important to be patient and give your spells time to work their magick before you declare them a dud. Smaller, less complicated spells can take days to get going, and bigger, farther-reaching spells might unfold over the course of weeks, months, or even years!

If you write a spell, perform it, wait ten minutes, proclaim it didn't work, and then move on to something else, you're doing yourself a disservice. It might have performed exactly as expected if you had just given it time to show you its results!

Tip #4: Know what you're expecting beforehand.

I spoke about this at length in chapter two, but it's worth reiterating. Before you begin creating your spell, you need to get really specific and spell out what you're hoping the spell will accomplish. That intention needs to be crystal clear!

During the writing process, this will help keep all your efforts focused and on track. But after testing the spell, this intention will give you a clear benchmark to gauge your success.

This is particularly important because as spell writers there's the temptation to fudge our success. You've worked so hard on your spell that you just can't bear to see it fail—so when it comes time to examine the results, you're tempted to view them through rose-colored glasses.

Having a specific intention that has guided the entire process of spell writing will make it more of a challenge to see your results as anything other than what they actually are.

Tip #5: Don't stop trying, and don't stop testing!

It's no secret that we experience disappointment when things don't work out like we were planning. When your spell doesn't function like you intend it to, it's normal to feel discouraged and question your abilities as a spell writer and witch.

But when it comes to this art, those negative results you see are actually a beneficial thing! When a spell flops, that's a sign that something about it just wasn't working out. If you're measuring your results like you should be, it likely will be easy to locate the culprit and avoid it going forward. This was an opportunity to close a door that leads to a magickal dead end.

Your spell may not have worked, but it absolutely improved in the process!

So—especially when you're starting out—don't be too hard on yourself if every spell you write doesn't go as planned. It's part of the process, and that process is improving your skills, even though it might feel discouraging at the time.

Pick yourself up, record your findings, and use them to create an even better spell than before!

CORRESPONDENCE TABLES

What follows are some of my personal correspondences that I consider to be the most important and fundamental to my spell writing. This is by no means a complete list of possible correspondences, but they have proven to be a solid foundation for my magick, and I hope that they will benefit you as well.

Unlike some tables you'll find, I've done my best to provide at least some brief explanation of how and why these correspondences are used the way they are. I find that this format allows you to gain a deeper understanding of each, while still allowing for quick and easy reference in the heat of spell writing!

CHAPTER 6: COLOR CORRESPONDENCES

I n this chapter, we're taking a look at some of the color correspondences I like to use when writing my own spells. However, you should always keep in mind that magick is not an exact science—what works for one witch won't necessarily be as effective for another. I recommend that you use these correspondences as a jumping off point.

As you progress in your own spell writing abilities, you'll discover that firsthand, personal experience is the best indicator of which correspondences work for you. So, don't be afraid to experiment with different colors to better understand how they influence the flow of spiritual energy in your spells.

White

White is the color of purity and newness. It evokes the power of positivity and divine light within the universe.

Because of these connotations, white is a good candle color when you're working spells that have to do with blessing or consecrating. Similarly, it's a good, general color to use when invoking or communicating with Gods and Goddesses. It's true that different deities have different colors associated with them, but if you're unsure of what shade to use, white is a safe bet.

Similarly, white candles are a good replacement when you are unable to find candles that are more unusual colors. You should always try your best to match hues exactly, but sometimes there's just not a topaz or a periwinkle candle to be found! In these instances, white acts a nice blank slate upon which numerous types of spiritual energy can be projected.

Black

Black is a color that often unfairly gets associated with scary, bad things. But within Wicca, black is a positive and important color!

This dark hue is a symbol of banishment and protection. We burn black candles to keep unfriendly spirits at bay—not to invite them in! Black is also the right choice for keeping negativity away in general.

Additionally, black can be used for spells about breaking bad habits or moving on from a difficult chapter in your life. It's a color that both marks the end of something but also implies a new beginning.

Red

Like I mentioned earlier, most all of us associate red with love. However, red more generally represents passion of any kind—not just romantic passion. It's a color that's all about achieving your dreams and pursuing the things that excite you.

If we go further and break red down into different hues, I would say that light red or pink is best for magick about love and physical attraction. Bright red is good for health and vitality (as it's the color of blood), and dark red should be reserved for spells about courage and motivation.

Finally, red is a color that's associated with both the winter and summer solstices—two of the most important holidays on the Wiccan calendar. In the winter, it represents the red berries of evergreen plants, and in the summer, it represents the fiery power of the sun.

Blue

Blue is the color of mystery and mysticism. We see this association in nature—both in the mysterious, murky depths of the deep blue sea and the expansive, unfathomable blue-black cosmos.

This color is best suited for magick that has to do with psychic abilities or communication with spirits, as both of these things are highly mystical. Additionally, burning a blue candle before bed can help foster symbolic, prophetic dreams.

But really, anything to do with spirituality can benefit from the presence of a blue candle!

Yellow

Yellow, like red, is highly associated with our sun. And as the sun gives life to everything on the planet, the color yellow will invigorate and enlighten your magick.

Use this vibrant color when your magick deals with things like creativity, planning for the future, or making a positive change in your life. In these instances, it can also help to pair a yellow candle with a black one so that you're simultaneously bringing in light and life and banishing negativity and darkness.

Orange

Orange is a color that draws attention to itself—it's so bright and vibrant that it's hard to miss! And orange is perfect for when you want to harness some of that in-your-face-energy.

Use orange when working spells that have to do with friendship or other social interactions. Developing charisma, becoming a better public speaker, making a good first impression, and other similar goals will benefit from the presence of orange.

Purple

Purple is a contemplative color. This is not the hue you turn to when you want to take action or make huge changes—it's the color you turn to when you want to sit and think.

Because of these associations, purple corresponds highly with both wisdom and prayer. When you've got a difficult decision to make and want to make the right choice, consider purple. When you want to strengthen the bonds between yourself and the divine, choose purple. If you're worried about your academic performance, choose purple.

It's a hue that contains all the wisdom of the ages.

Green

Green is the color of the earth and of natural life. It represents the connection between humans and their environment. As such, spells involving plants or the earth absolutely need the presence of green.

However, green is also a shade that invokes feelings of tranquility and peace—think of how relaxing the sound of a gentle wind blowing through the trees is. So, turn to green when you're feeling stressed and need to unwind as well.

Silver

Silver is the color of the moon, and it embodies all the power of our celestial mother. This is the color you should turn to when working magick associated with the Triple Goddess—our primary conception of divine feminine power within Wicca.

Like the color blue, silver is also good for magick that involves psychic abilities or making contact with the great beyond. Any sort of spiritual wisdom will be enhanced by the presence of a silver candle.

Gold

Gold equals royalty and wealth in the non-Wiccan world, and those associations hold true within witchcraft as well.

Even though it represents prosperity, keep in mind that this doesn't always mean material prosperity. Gold can also help you cultivate a rich inner life or a wealth of friends and family. Additionally, you should turn to gold when you need to be a strong, just leader—it can help with promoting fairness and insight.

CHAPTER 7: NUMBER CORRESPONDENCES

E ven though we might not all be math whizzes, the world of witchcraft still realizes that numbers are more than squiggles on a page—they are powerful symbols and correspondences that can help shape and strengthen our will and intention in subtle and unexpected ways.

Zero

The number zero is probably one of the most enigmatic and paradoxical of all the numbers in existence—it represents nothingness, yet the circle used to depict it is most definitely something, not nothing.

This is also one number that shows up naturally in most types of witchcraft in the form of a circle. We perform most of our rituals within the protection of the sacred circle, but in a way, that shape also represents a zero. Physically, within the bounds of the circle there is nothing, yet when we begin our rituals, magick appears out of that nothing.

And that's the true power of the number zero—it's the void, the nothingness that life miraculously springs from. It's Divine will made manifest from thin air. And when you really stop to think about it, that's a truly magickal thought.

One

If zero represents nothing, then the number one most definitely represents everything. It is a symbol of the perfect union of the universe. One embodies all of the dualities of life—male and female, life and death, sun and moon, up and down, etc.

Because of its unified nature, the number one is a sign of cooperation and synthesis. If two or more witches are performing a ritual, it can be good to have one center of focus (like a singular candle) for everyone involved to direct their will and intention.

However, one can be interpreted as a lone number as well. For the solitary witch, this number can symbolize personal autonomy, free thinking, and taking the road less traveled.

Two

Two is obviously another number closely related to union and duality. But I still conceive of it as being subtly different from the unified nature of the number one.

With the number one, many parts meld into a unified whole until they can no longer be distinguished from one another. However, with the number two, those parts may still be working towards the same goal, but they are symbolized as distinct, independent entities. Therefore, two is very much a number related to cooperation and mutual respect. It is a number to turn to when trying to resolve a conflict.

The number two is also a representation of the dual nature of Divinity. It encapsulates both the God and the Goddess with their cooperative masculine and feminine energies. When invoking the Divine in broad terms (as opposed to specific deities), burn two candles to honor this dualistic configuration.

Three

Both inside and outside the world of witchcraft, the number three is considered a lucky and highly important number. It represents spiritual wisdom and the realm of Divine knowledge. Three is the number of psychics, seers, and others trying to know and experience the unseen forces at work all around us.

It is also a number of attraction—when used correctly, the number three can draw positive spiritual energy towards yourself and into your sacred circle. It takes a very active role in the world of magick.

For Wiccans in particular, three also represents the Triple Goddess—the personification of the Divine feminine as Mother, Maiden, and Crone.

Four

There are four primal elements commonly recognized in witchcraft—earth, air, fire, and water. This tie to the natural realm makes four a number of pragmatism and physical energy. Additionally, the concept of the four quarters or four winds (north, south, east, and west) plays a big role in magick as well.

Four is also a number of stability and architecture—think of the four sides of a square. So, when planning out rituals that are complicated or have a lot of moving parts, consider using groupings of four to provide a natural structure to the proceedings.

Five

Five is another highly symbolic number in witchcraft because it represents the five points of the pentagram. Typically, the lower four points correspond to the four elements, while the topmost point represents Spirit or Divinity.

However, in some traditions, the number five is not as wholesome or complete. Instead, it can represent struggle or chaos—or more broadly, the seemingly random nature of life. But this does not at all meant that five is a negative number.

For example, in Celtic witchcraft, five could symbolize the ritual struggle between the Oak King and Holly King across the wheel of the year. Additionally, five is a number of importance for practitioners of chaos magick—a spiritual tradition where unpredictability and unorthodox methods are prioritized.

Six

While three is a number of attraction, six is most definitely a number of banishment.

The hexagram (or six-pointed star) is most commonly associated with Judaism as the Star of David, but it has importance in occult practices as well. Most commonly, it's used as a talisman to ward off evil spirits or negative energy. This may have to do with the legend of the Seal of Solomon—an ancient, magickal ring with an engraved hexagram that was said to contain the power to cast out demons.

Seven

Seven is a number associated with the Divine feminine energy of the moon. As such, it is a number of comfort and protection. It's similar in this sense to the number six, but unlike it, the power of seven is maternal and loving, not fierce and aggressive.

In addition to the Divine, seven is also a symbol of dreams and other forms of esoteric, mystery knowledge. So, be on the lookout when the number seven or groups of seven appear to you during sleep. This is a major sign of something important.

Eight

The number eight embodies all the wonder and power of the cycle of life—birth, life, death, and rebirth. Just as it is depicted with a symbol made of one continuous, infinite line, it represents the forward march of life as it rises, falls, and rises again.

Because of this close association with the wheel of life, eight is not always a number of pleasantness and goodness—death is a part of that process after all. However, it does encourage us to accept the inevitable flow of the universe with clear-minded dignity. And it reminds us that, with the infinite, there is no stopping point. Death cannot be the end of something constantly in flux.

Additionally, in the Wiccan tradition, there are generally eight *Sabbats* (major holidays) per year, so this number is associated particularly with the ceremonies and rituals that accompany them.

Nine

Because it is a multiple of three, nine is another number with strong ties to the Divine feminine, particularly the Crone aspect of the Triple Goddess. Therefore, the number nine represents wisdom, experience, and power that only advanced age can bring to a witch.

When working a ritual that deals with making a difficult decision or with personal uncertainty, turn to the number nine. It can help guide you towards the correct path you need to take.

CHAPTER 8: MOON PHASE CORRESPONDENCES

E ach month, the moon moves through phases. These different phases of the moon can influence your magick in powerful ways, depending on your specific purposes. The spiritual energy of the moon aligns strongly with different types of spells at different points in the month, and as a spell writer you can use this to your advantage.

The New Moon

When no light from the sun is reflecting off the moon and it looks mysteriously absent from our sky, this is known as the new (or dark) moon. However, just because the moon may not be visible at this point doesn't mean it's not still working its magick!

This particular phase is a great time for banishment rituals. From ridding your mind of negative thoughts or habits to banishing bad energy from a home, this sort of magick should be saved for the new moon. The dark face of the moon during this time is charged with the power to absorb and dispel any negative spiritual forces you may be facing.

Additionally, the new moon is an appropriate time for magick meant to honor the dead or communicate with spirits. The barrier between our world and the next is at its weakest on nights when the moon doesn't shine. Always perform rituals involving the dead with the utmost caution—since this point is the time when the spiritual barrier is the weakest, it also is the time of the month when spirits are at their strongest.

The Waxing Moon

Although it begins as nothing more than a sliver, during the waxing phase of the moon it grows stronger and brighter. This is a time of new life and new beginnings, and your magick during this period should reflect that. For example, the blessing of a child, a handfasting ceremony (a Pagan wedding), or coven initiation rites should all take place during the waxing moon.

If you're a solitary practitioner, the waxing moon is also a good time to formally begin your studies. Performing an initiation or seeker ritual during this time will get your journey started on the right foot.

(If you're interested in learning more about initiation rites for solitary witches, be sure to check out my book *The Ritual Magick Manual*.)

Basically, any spells or rituals involving growth or the start of something new will benefit from the waxing moon.

The Full Moon

Most of society might associate the full moon with werewolves, but for witches, it's a bit more of a positive thing! As the moon is associated with Divine feminine power (more on that in the next chapter), this is the point in the month when the Goddess is at her peak. She is ready and willing to bestow blessings during a full moon.

As such, this is a great time for purification rituals or other blessings. The light of a full moon consecrates everything it touches, so you'll want to take advantage of it while it lasts. This can range from simply placing an object you want to bless outdoors during a full moon to a more elaborate blessing ritual, like the one we'll be looking at a little later in this book.

The full moon is also a good time for magick of protection. While the energy of the new moon banishes negativity, the energy of the full moon draws in positivity and light. Think of the moon as our celestial mother—she's watching over and protecting us from above.

Finally, fertility rites are also appropriate during the full moon. Since this is the point in the month where the spirit world is saturated with Divine feminine power, it only makes sense that this would be beneficial for childbearing.

The Waning Moon

As the moon enters the last leg of its journey, it is known as the waning moon. It's at this point it moves from bright fullness back to dark nothingness. However, this doesn't mean it's any less spiritually potent during this phase—it's simply that its energies are aligning with different types of magick.

In particular, the waning moon is the perfect time to develop your psychic or divination skills. There is much mystery and wisdom in the moon as it enters old age, so it has much to teach you. This is also the right time of the month for magick relating to dreaming or prophecy.

During the fall months, the waning moon is also a time reserved for offerings of thanksgiving to the Gods for a good harvest.

Lunar Eclipses

While they might be more common than solar eclipses, a lunar eclipse isn't something you see every day. That's why it holds particular magickal significance.

Many of the correspondences associated with the new moon are enhanced and intensified during a lunar eclipse. So, it's a particularly good time for banishment magick—especially when dealing with malevolent entities.

Really, any kind of magick involving spirits, human or otherwise, is going to be at its most potent during a total lunar eclipse. Channeling, necromancy, and exorcisms will all work well during this time. However, I urge you to proceed with extreme caution when attempting powerful rituals like these.

Finally, lunar eclipses are a good time to honor Goddesses associated with the dark of the moon. These include figures like Hecate, Tiamat, and Lilith. Although fearsome, these powerful feminine deities are at the height of their power during an eclipse and are willing to lend a hand to the worthy.

Blue Moons

In a normal year, we have 12 full moons. But from time to time, a 13th annual moon shows up. To figure out which moon during one of these years is the blue moon, you have to look at the four seasons. Typically, each season will have three full moons. When a season has four, the third moon of the season is known as the blue moon.

In more recent times, the term "blue moon" has come to refer to a month that has two full moons. While this is common usage, witches traditionally stick to the older definition of the blue moon, since it ties into the changing of the seasons and the cycle of life.

Because they're so unique, blue moons are an incredibly powerful sign of good luck. If you want to work spells that involve prosperity or material wealth, schedule them for a blue moon. You're not going to have a luckier night of the year!

CHAPTER 9: PLANT CORRESPONDENCES

C hoosing herbs and plants that complement your magickal rituals will increase their potency. But if you have difficulty finding a particular item in this list, don't let it worry you too much. Strong correspondences enhance your magick, but ultimately, that magick originates from your intention. Substitutions are fine, if you can find a plant with similar correspondences.

Apple

They might not be the most exotic fruit, but they are a good one nonetheless. Apples represent abundance, generosity, and the bounty of the earth. Before growing season, bless your garden by sprinkling apple skins across the dirt.

Basil

This common herb is good for money spells and prosperity magick. Slip a leaf in your wallet or purse to help attract good fortune. Basil is also useful for burnt offerings.

Blackberry

Blackberries represent bravery and admiration. They also make a good offering when invoking a God or Goddess.

Cedar

There's something heavenly about the smell of a cedar tree. And for good reason too—it's closely associated with the Divine. Cedar is a smart choice if you're looking to communicate with deities or spirits. A ring of cedar chips or shavings is also known to consecrate and protect the space inside the circle.

Cardamom

This fragrant spice is good for rest and relaxation—both physically and emotionally. Use it when you're looking for peace of mind or struggling with anger.

Daffodil

These bright, beautiful flowers are the color of our sun, and as such, they represent vitality and prosperity. They're perfect for spells about achieving your goals or advancing in a career.

Dandelion

They may be considered weeds, but dandelions have important magickal qualities. They represent goodness, honesty, and virtue and can help signal good intentions when dealing with deities or other metaphysical beings.

Dogwood

Dogwood blossoms are closely associated with creativity and artistic ability. Dogwood petals can be used to bless objects of creativity, like musical instruments or canvases. A branch from a dogwood tree can be fashioned into a wand that's ideal for a drawing down the moon ritual.

Fennel

This bulbous plant and stringy herb are ideal for weather-related magic. An offering of fennel can bring much-needed rains or keep severe weather at bay.

Forget-Me-Not

Like the name implies, forget-me-nots are loosely associated with memory. They make a good flower for rituals to commemorate the dead, but they can also be used to help come to terms with difficult events in your past.

Ginger

Turn to ginger if you're looking for charm, articulation, and people skills. It can be incorporated into rituals, but you can also just give it a good chew before a big presentation or a first date.

Goldenrod

These flowers make a good addition to rituals about protection and guidance. Use goldenrod to get in touch with your guardian angel or spirit guide.

Green Onion

They might be pungent, but green onions are ideal for all things related to dreams. Whether you want to improve your dream interpretation skills, remember your dreams more clearly, or experience symbolic dreams, green onions are the way to go.

Honeysuckle

It's fragrant, tasty, and spiritually powerful. Honeysuckle should be incorporated into your spring equinox celebration because of its associations with vegetation, growth, and new life. Other uses of honeysuckle include initiation rites, holiday celebrations, and consecration rituals.

Lavender

This fragrant and beautiful flower is associated with psychic and spiritual wisdom. It is imbued with Divine knowledge and is perfect for sages, seers, and prophets.

Lily

White lilies are a sign of deep love and devotion. They make a welcome addition to handfasting rituals (Wiccan weddings), but they can also be used in love spells and potions. Lilies may also represent purification and innocence.

Mint

The herb with a kick, mint is a symbol of good luck and serendipity. Additionally, sleeping with a sprig under your pillow is thought to bring prophetic dreams.

Mustard

Mustard seeds are a perfect fit for traditional healing magick. They absorb negative energy into themselves, storing it safely inside. After using mustard seeds in a ritual be sure to dispose of them away from your home, in order to avoid re-encountering that bad energy.

Nutmeg

Nutmeg has psychedelic properties—although I strongly advise against ingesting it. However, it can still be useful in rituals involving higher planes of existence. Communicating with beings on a higher vibrational level can be enhanced with nutmeg.

Oak

Oak trees live long lives, and because of this, they are very wise. That's why they are symbols of intuition and knowledge. Their wisdom is not something you learn from books—it's wisdom that can only be learned by listening to the trees.

Oregano

Turn to oregano if you're looking for focus and mental clarity. Burning oregano before a ritual can help center your thoughts and solidify your intention.

Pepper

Peppers are good for rituals that involve generating large amounts of spiritual energy—this could be anything from invocations to chanting mantras. All varieties will enhance your efforts, but the spicier the better. Just be sure to take precautions when handling them!

Rose

These flowers may be associated with love, but really, they represent passion of any kind. Roses are a friend of the ambitious and the dreamers. White roses in particular have associations with the Triple Goddess.

Rosemary

Rosemary is the herb to use when dealing with difficult people. It fosters empathy and goodwill. It's also a good fragrance to incorporate into meditation and creative visualization.

Saffron

This bright red, costly herb holds all sorts of mystical value. Saffron is useful for lucid dreaming, astral projection, and past life regression. It can also be used in the blessing of a home or in fertility rites.

Sage

Sage is the classic herb used for cleansing and blessing. Burning sage inside a home wards off evil spirits and protects occupants from negative energies. Sleeping with sage under your mattress or pillow can also prevent nightmares.

Thyme

Turn to thyme for practical wisdom and making tough decisions. It can provide you the clarity of mind you need to see a situation for what it really is. Thyme is also a good choice for rituals to mend a broken heart.

Tulip

No matter the hue, tulips are good for happiness and positive energy. If you're looking for a fresh start and want to commemorate it with a ritual, be sure to include tulips. Additionally, bring a bouquet of tulips to your next housewarming party. It makes a beautiful gift for the recipient and will draw positive energy into their new home.

CHAPTER 10: DAY CORRESPONDENCES

The timing and date of your spells can be very important in witchcraft—however, I do recommend keeping your time-based correspondences to just one or two per spell.

The more you add on, the harder it will be to find a date that fits all the requirements. When you're frantically trying to find a new moon in December that falls on a Saturday with a date that ends in seven that happens before the Winter Solstice you'll see what I'm talking about!

Sunday

As the name implies, Sunday is the day of the sun. It is a predominantly masculine day, as the sun is the masculine counterpart of the feminine moon. Colors associated with Sunday include gold, yellow, white, and red.

If you're planning a ritual that involves material wealth, new beginnings, or physical power, consider performing it on a Sunday. This is particularly true when Sunday falls on the spring equinox or the summer solstice. Invoke the Gods Bast, Horus, Apollo, or other sun-based Gods on this day.

Monday

As the beginning of the work week, Monday represents vitality, growth, and good fortune. It contains a good balance of both feminine and masculine energies. Colors associated with Monday include green, red, and orange.

Try a ritual on Monday if you're seeking personal development, practical knowledge, or leadership skills. Gods associated with Mondays include Mammon, Krishna, Gad, and other fortune deities.

Tuesday

If Monday is a day of the practical, mundane world, then Tuesday is its polar opposite. It's a good day for divination and other psychic skills, and it is decidedly feminine. Colors associated with Tuesday include dark blue, purple, black, and silver. Like I mentioned before, Tuesdays are good for psychic development, but they're also suitable for related things—like prophecy, astral projection, and spiritual wisdom in general. For invocations, try Brigid, Sophia, Athena, or other wisdom Goddesses on a Tuesday.

Wednesday

Wednesdays are divine! If you have an invocation ritual to perform, you will rarely go wrong planning it for a Wednesday. Whether you have a petition or simply want to show a God or Goddess honor, this is the prime day for it.

Colors associated with Wednesday include silver, gold, royal purple, and bright red. Invocations aside, Wednesdays are also a good choice for rituals with a heavy emphasis on elemental magick. Gods and Goddesses of all kinds can be invoked on Wednesdays.

Thursday

By Thursday, the week is half over—things are beginning to wind down. That's why Thursday has such a strong association with things like peace, tranquility, and friendship. Thursdays are another day that's strongly feminine, but there may be a little bit more masculine in the mix than on a Tuesday.

Colors associated with Thursday include pink, lavender, earth tones, and off-white. On Thursdays, invoke Concordia, Harmonia, or other peace deities—especially Goddesses.

Friday

Fridays are associated with art, creativity, and other intellectual pursuits—it is a day of spiritual nourishment and imagination. This particular day is another one that's equal parts feminine and masculine.

Colors associated with Fridays include orange, light blue, dark red, indigo, and yellow. Call upon Minerva, Dionysus, Odin, Gwydion, and other Gods and Goddesses of art on Fridays.

Saturday

Saturday is a day of remembrance for the dead. As such, rituals involving communicating with spirits, exorcisms, or funeral rites are naturally suited for this day.

Colors associated with Saturday are black predominantly, but also gray, green, brown, and dark purple. On Saturdays, invoke death deities like Ereshkigal, Anubis, Osiris, and Orcus.

CHAPTER 11: WICCAN HOLIDAY CORRESPONDENCES

A lthough it may sound unexpected, we witches know how to party.

Now, you probably won't find many of us doing keg stands or dancing the night away at the club, but the fact remains that we enjoy a good celebration. And that's why we take our holidays so seriously.

What follows in this chapter is a look at the eight major holidays, or *Sabbats*, that mark the high points on the Wiccan calendar. Each one has its own different flavor and purpose, but they all add up to a yearly celebration of life and spiritual power.

Writing holiday-specific spells can be a great way to get in on the celebration and hone your skills, so I highly recommend finding an upcoming Sabbat and marking the occasion with your own unique magickal offering!

The Winter Solstice

Also known as Yule or Midwinter, the winter solstice is the official unofficial beginning of the Wiccan year. It's one of the most ancient holidays in all of humankind, for Wiccans and non-Wiccans alike. Researchers speculate that the winter solstice has been celebrated in some form or another since at least the Stone Age!

Astronomically, the winter solstice marks the time of year when nighttime is longest and daytime is the shortest. For those of us who love the long, chilly winter nights, it's doesn't get much better than this.

But Yule is about so much more than this particular point in the earth's journey around the sun. Spiritually, it commemorates the movement from death into rebirth in the cycle of life. Think about it: this is the time of year when not much is growing in the natural world. The fields are cold and empty, and not much besides the heartiest of plants can survive.

However, this bleakness doesn't last—since the beginning of time, this period of dark and cold has always been followed by sunnier, livelier days. But we don't get to those without passing through the winter first. Yule is about honoring this time of darkness as an essential part in the ever-turning wheel of life.

The winter solstice is the perfect time for working magick about banishment. If you've got bad habits you want to drop or painful memories you want to move on from, this is the right holiday to begin that journey.

Although the dates vary from year to year, the winter solstice typically falls somewhere near December 20th.

Imbolg

Also known as Imbolc or Brigid, this holiday falls on February 1st. At this point in the year, we're still in the throes of winter, but by this time, spring is well on its way! And it's the perfect holiday for meditating on and preparing for this upcoming season of life.

While the winter solstice may be a good time for banishing bad habits, Imbolg is the right time to begin new ones. Similarly, if there are positive things in your life that may have fallen to the wayside, this holiday is the perfect time to rededicate yourself to those things.

Finally, Imbolg is the right time to begin that oh-so-dreaded yearly ritual of spring cleaning. So, spruce up your home altar if you've got one and organize your tools to ensure that everything is in order when those sunnier months roll around...and they'll be here quicker than you might think!

The Spring Equinox

At the spring (or vernal) equinox, spring is finally here! Like the winter solstice, the exact day will vary from year to year, but it typically falls around March 20th. Astronomically, this is one of the two days on the calendar when daytime and nighttime are completely equal in length.

Spiritually, this is a holiday of new life and the blessings that go along with it. So, pull out any tools that need to be consecrated and seal them with spiritual power at this time.

The spring equinox is also the time when some Wiccans and other Pagans celebrate and honor the goddess Ostara—in some traditions, this holiday is named after her. Ostara is depicted as a young, beautiful maiden, which is fitting, since at this time of year the earth is in the same condition. She, like the holiday, represents newness, innocence and purity, which is why I recommend blessing rituals at this time.

Flowers and other beautiful signs of life are a must for the equinox, so don't be afraid to fill your home to the gills with these symbols of regeneration.

Beltane

Falling on April 30th or May 1st, Beltane (or May Day) is another occasion to surround yourself with plenty of beautiful flowers and other plants. However, this is a holiday that is also specifically associated with fertility.

But before you go out and buy a basinet, keep in mind that fertility can be about more than just childbirth. This is the time of year when the ground is at its most fertile, and many crops are planted on or around Beltane. Even if you don't have much of a green thumb yourself, it's the perfect holiday to honor the earth and the life-giving bounty that she is about to provide for us.

The Summer Solstice

The summer solstice (aka Midsummer or Litha) is the polar opposite of the winter solstice. This is the day when the sun is at the peak of its powers—daylight is longest, while nighttime is shortest.

Because of this association with the sun, we honor it and the God (which corresponds to it) at this time. Be sure to honor him with a gift of flowers or other plants to show your appreciation for his life-giving light.

This is also the holiday when Wiccans are the most likely to get a little wild and crazy. We want to honor and respect the sun at this holiday, but there's no reason that it can't be done with a little joyful partying!

The summer solstice date will vary, but it falls somewhere around June 20th each year.

Lammas

Lammas (also known as Lughnasadah) is a late-summer festival that falls on August 1st. And it can be downright frightening.

In the olden days, crops were not quite ready to harvest at this point in the year, but they were well on their way. Even if things looked promising, farmers always had the fear in the back of their minds that it wouldn't be enough to keep their families afloat during the cold winter months.

However, instead of running from their fears, they created an entire holiday about them! Similarly, Lammas is a good time for you to face your own fears. Is there something you've been putting off this year? Now is the time to begin! Is there something in your life that frightens you? Bring it out into the open on Lammas to deprive it of its power!

There are lots of things to be scared of in this world, but when we set aside time like this to face them head on with a clear mind, we actually get the upper hand over them.

The Autumn Equinox

Like the spring equinox, the autumn equinox (or Mabon) is a time of balance. Once again on this day, light and darkness come in equal measure. However, unlike in the spring, we approach this holiday knowing that the sun is in its decline and close to being replaced by the darkness of winter. But once again, we honor this time of year as essential to the never-ending cycle of life.

Mabon is a time for giving thanks—for a successful harvest, for friends and family, for the beautiful changing colors of the leaves, and everything in between. If you have anything in your life that you're grateful for, the autumn equinox is the time to make your thanks known.

The date of this holiday varies, but it will fall each year sometime close to September 20th.

Samhain

The rest of the world may know it as Halloween, but for Wiccans, October 31st will always be Samhain.

While there's nothing wrong with having fun with ghosts, goblins, jack-o-lanterns, and plenty of candy, this holiday is actually of the utmost importance for witches. It is the point in the year when we give honor to loved ones who are no longer here with us. Death is a natural part of life, and on Samhain, we remember those who have completed their life's journey before us.

Visiting the graves of loved ones or burning a candle in their memory are two common ways that Wiccans commemorate the dead, but even if that's not possible, simply taking some time on this day to reminisce and think of good times gone by can bring honor to your departed friends or family members.

Samhain is also the time of year when the natural world and the spiritual world are in closest communion. Many witches take advantage of this fact by using this time for magick that involves spirits of the dead or other spiritual beings.

CHAPTER 12: WRITE FROM THE HEART AND LET THE SPIRIT GUIDE YOU

Performing spells is one of the most thrilling aspects of witchcraft, but even it can't beat the great feeling you get from lovingly and carefully crafting a spell all of your very own. It's been a pleasure to experience your first steps into the world of spell writing, and I hope you've learned some useful things from this book!

Spell writing is a sacred art, no doubt, but as you've read these pages, you've hopefully discovered that it's supposed to be a fun, liberating process as well. Humanity's capability for creativity and imagination keeps us in communion with the divine spirit of the universe—and using magick as an outlet for that creativity is never a boring experience!

As you continue down this enchanted path of spell writing, remember that perseverance is the most important skill you need to develop. No amount of technical knowledge about magick will ever be able to rival the gumption of a determined witch. Keep experimenting, keep learning, and most importantly, keep making magick—our failures only bring us that much closer to success!

If you enjoyed what you read, I invite you to investigate my new website, ExploreWicca.com. It's full of long-form, original spells and articles meant to instruct and enrich you spiritually. And best of all, the content you'll find there is absolutely free. Stop by today—I love having new visitors!

Finally, I would be extremely grateful for an honest review of the book. I want to provide my readers with spells and magickal rituals that are important and useful to them, and receiving your feedback is one way I can better serve you.

Blessed Be,

Didi

CHAPTER 13: READ MORE FROM DIDI CLARKE

The Wiccan Bible for the Solitary Witch

Are you a spiritual seeker who marches to the beat of your own drum? Are you looking to explore the world of Wicca while still maintaining your independent spirit?

The Wiccan Bible for the Solitary Witch is the ultimate resource for learning the fundamentals of witchcraft as a freethinking, solo practitioner!

Didi Clarke has been studying the art of Wicca for over a decade as a solitary witch, and in that time, she's published numerous books about all aspects of the craft. She has an intimate knowledge of the joys and pitfalls of studying Wicca without the aid of a coven. Now that expertise can be yours too!

In *The Wiccan Bible for the Solitary Witch*, you'll find easy-to-understand descriptions and explanations of the most important aspects of being a practicing Wiccan. Knowledge that was once a closely guarded secret of traditional covens can be yours to learn and apply to your own spiritual practice!

In particular, this book will teach you things like:
- Wiccan Ethics
- Important Wiccan Terms
- How Magick Works
- Wiccan Holidays
- How Wiccans Pray
- Writing Your Own Spells
- Performing Rituals
- And much more!

This information is a must-have if you're a solitary witch who wants to experience the liberating power of magick in your own life. It's a self-guided manual for anyone who values their unique perspective and wants to become a successful Wiccan!

Buy *The Wiccan Bible for the Solitary Witch* today!

The White Magick Spell Book

Unlock the Power of Light and Goodness in the World!

White magick is all about making the world a better place for yourself and all living creatures. Within the pages of *The White Magick Spell Book*, you'll find the rituals, spells, and information you need to make this better world a reality!

To some extent, we're all born with a natural desire to practice compassion towards other living things. But you'll find that as you delve deeper into this branch of witchcraft that your compassion will begin to grow even more, until being a help to others is second nature. White magick has many practical benefits, but I you'll find that the most important one is the transformation that takes place within your soul!

What You'll Find

Each of the spells you'll find in *The White Magick Spell Book* are broken down into easy, step-by-step instructions with plenty of explanatory notes to guide you through the process. It's important to understand the "why" of magick just as much as the "how."

However, it's my hope that these spells and rituals will help to expand the spiritual horizons of even the most experienced witch. They're all one-of-a-kind, original creations based on my own observations in the craft—you won't find these spells anywhere else!

When you read *The White Magick Spell Book*, you'll find a wide variety of magick meant to spread light and life. These include:

- Home Protection
- Emotional Healing
- Banishing Negativity
- Communicating with Guardian Angels
- Building Friendships
- And Much More!

The World of White Magick Awaits You!

Are you ready to experience all the benefits that white magick has to offer? Then buy *The White Magick Spell Book* today and witness its power for yourself!

The Wiccan Handbook of Candle Spells

Are you ready to tap into the magickal power of candles?

The Wiccan Handbook of Candle Spells is the ultimate resource for learning and practicing the art of candle magick!

Didi Clarke has been a Wiccan practitioner for over a decade, and in that time, she's published numerous books about all aspects of the craft. In The Wiccan Handbook of Candle Spells she shares her personal secrets for unlocking the spiritual power of the element of fire!

When you try these one-of-a-kind spells for yourself, you'll understand why candles are one of your most powerful tools as a witch. The Wiccan Handbook of Candle Spells is here to teach you things like:

- Candle blessings
- Banishing negativity
- Invoking deities
- Communication with the spirit world
- And much more!

In addition to original spells, this book is also a resource for understanding the philosophy behind candle magick. It's a one-stop guide to learning both the "how" and "why" of candle spells!

Whether you're new to the world of Wicca or are an experienced witch, *The Wiccan Handbook of Candle Spells* has something for you! These rituals pack serious power, but they're presented in an easy-to-understand, step-by-step format. Candle magick is an exciting, must-have tool for witches of all levels!

Buy The Wiccan Handbook of Candle Spells today!

Find me on Twitter at **@AuthorDidi**
And be sure to like my **Facebok page: facebook.com/authordidiclarke**
You can contact me via email at **authordidiclarke@gmail.com**

Printed in Great Britain
by Amazon

30942483R00040